Beauty
and
Her Beast

Romantic Poetry

by

N.R. Hart

Copyright © 2019 N.R.Hart
Copyright © 2019 Monday Creek Publishing
Cover Art by Logan Rogers
Cover Design by Gina McKnight
N.R.Hart logo design by R.A. Cantu
Duplication in any form, electronic or otherwise, is prohibited by law.
All rights reserved.
ISBN: 978-0-578-61644-5

"Maybe she needed someone to show her how to live and he needed someone to show him how to love."
– N.R.Hart

There was a girl and there was a beast and this is their love story...
– N.R.Hart

A Winter Season

"It takes a soft heart to
love this hard."

N.R.Hart

> I am the girl who loves too hard
> too long and too much.
> I am the girl who stays and stays
> because I know what it feels like
> to lose the rarest of loves.
> I am the girl who above all
> craves the deepest kind
> of soul love.
> I am the girl who is driven
> by love and love alone.
> And, I am the girl who walks
> through the fire for love.
> I will always be the girl who
> is a slave to this kind of love.
> God help me, I am that girl.

N.R. HART "DRIVEN BY LOVE" ©2019

And, we are all
a little broken
my darlings,
we just need
to find the one
who will keep
our pieces
safe with them.

—N.R.Hart "safe"

It was the kind of love
that could not be
explained.
It was all these feelings
with no name.
Maybe that is what love
is...
Something unexplainable.
Something that brings you
back home.
Something that makes you
feel more like yourself
in all the places
you never had a name
for...until now.

—N.R. Hart "home"©

"Every Beauty needs
her Beast
to protect her
from everything
but him."

N.R.HART

I am a bookish girl
I want intellect
and words
and poetry
lots of poetry
I want to fall in love
with your mind
seduce me with your
vocabulary
I want love stories
and romance
hot novels with wild
butterflies
and falling stars and love.
Especially love.

-N.R.Hart "bookish girl"

He felt her bury her head
into the crook of his neck
as he circled his arm
around her...
they stayed there for
the longest time
breathing to the safe sound
of their hearts pounding
for each other.

    N.R. Hart

I thought this time you would
love me
this time would be
different...
So I let my guard down
and, loved you even more.
And still, you didn't keep me
safe
and still, you didn't love me
at all...
Instead, you just watched me
stumble.
Instead, you just watched me fall.

-N.R.Hart "This time"

Contradiction

Strong yet vulnerable
how I adore each
side of you...
like a contradiction
a puzzle to be solved
I crave all these hidden
parts of you...
leaving me wanting more.
You always seem to know
what I want, what I need
and know how to give me
what I'm afraid to ask for.

—N.R.Hart

She was just a girl
who loved with her
whole heart
And, he was just a boy
who couldn't decide
from the start.

-N.R.Hart "Love Story"

Dream

There are some days
I need to escape
this world
and disappear from reality
in my dreams
I am running to you
you always meet me
there.
      -N.R.Hart ©

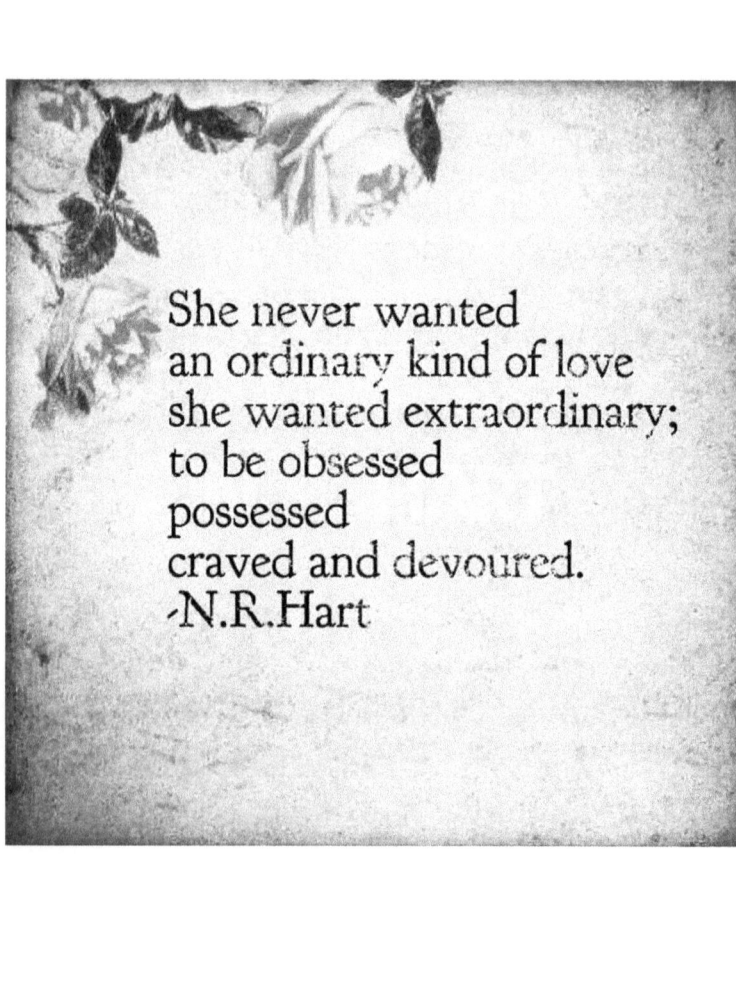

She never wanted
an ordinary kind of love
she wanted extraordinary;
to be obsessed
possessed
craved and devoured.
-N.R.Hart

And, sometimes she
scares him
really scares him
by how much she feels...
he didn't know
if he was capable
of being loved
in this way...
so unconditionally
so shamelessly, so wildly
loved.

-N.R.Hart "wildly loved" ©

Found

Sometimes the thought of you
I hold my breath with how much
I miss you...
Like we are on two worlds
always reaching and reaching
and never touching...
I need to find you and touch you
I need for you to find me
because I am right here where
you left me...
You don't need maps only our hands
to reach out and tear away at our distance.
You have always found me before.
And I am always waiting to be found.
By you.

    -N.R.Hart

It was so tender the way
she held onto him
always touching him...
his arm his sleeve his hand
as if she were about
to lose him at any moment...
she held on tight to
anything
she could get her hands on
and she often wonders...
how he could so carelessly
loosen his grip and let her
slip through his.

-N.R.Hart "hands"

I miss you.
I miss everything about you.
I miss being with you.
Laughing with you.
The feeling of excitement
knowing I would soon see you.
I miss the way time was motionless
when we were together.
I never cared about time when
I was with you.
I miss you at midnight.
I miss you at eight o'clock
in the morning when you
would send a funny text.
I miss every text message
from you.
I was waiting to see you again.
I always thought I would see you
again.

-N.R.Hart "I Miss You" ©

i don't know but i need you
in my life
in ways even i do not
understand
not to keep breathing
but in ways that leave me
breathless.

-N.R.Hart

Love me harder

I am having some
trouble
feeling you today...
And, I don't know how
to not feel you...
I need you to love me
a little harder.

-N.R.Hart "Love me harder"©

I was even more
surprised
to discover
the truth...
that I was madly
hopelessly...
in love with you.

- N.R.Hart

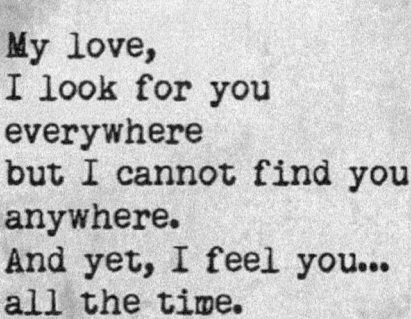

My love,
I look for you
everywhere
but I cannot find you
anywhere.
And yet, I feel you...
all the time.

-N.R.Hart

She's just an old soul
a die hard romantic
never giving up hope
even when there is none;
she's just a daydreamer
dwelling on poetry
and romance
and always, love.

-N.R.Hart, *author "poetry and pearls"*©

Once Upon A Time

Once upon a time
when you were mine...
we would laugh and play
a secret world away
and when I asked you
to stay
come what may...
But, you couldn't see
that we were meant to be
Once....
when you loved me.

-N.R.Hart

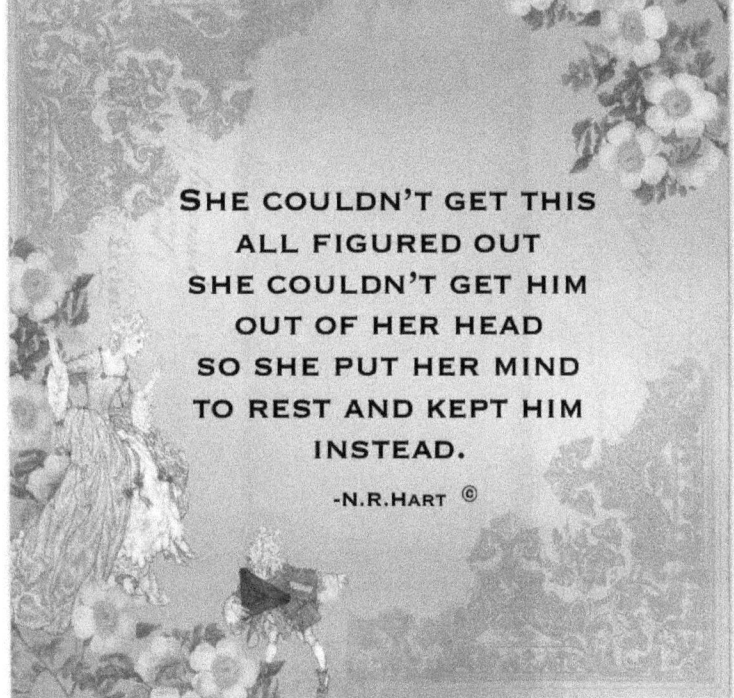

And, if I could be
your reflection
for just a moment...
look into my eyes
and see
the beauty I see
staring back at me.

-N.R.Hart "Reflection" ©2015

Alive

I try to convince myself
each day
I'm doing fine without
you
truth is...
I haven't been alive since
you've gone darling,
I'm barely breathing
at all.

        -N.R.Hart

What if I showed you
my darkness...
what if I showed you
my scars...
what if I told you
my secrets...
Would you still love me
then?
The real me. The one you
see.
Say you will love me...
Even then.

—N.R.Hart "say you will love me" ©2018

When they asked her
what was it about him
that made her feel
this way...
she could never really explain
what he did to her
she felt things with him
she had never felt before
with anyone.
She only knew that when she
was with him she was the
happiest
she had ever been.
And, it was as simple and as
complicated as that.

N.R.Hart

Our eyes searched
one another
for answers
when we weren't
even sure
of the questions.
We only knew that
our eyes
were peering
into our souls.

-N.R.Hart

"My soul thirsts for yours...
I needed you like I needed air to breathe.
From the moment our lips met you tasted like survival on me."

—N.R.Hart "Soulmate poem" © 2015

The invisible girl

You know her kind...she's the quiet type.
She doesn't say much but she thinks a lot
sometimes too much.
She is the one standing in the corner blending
in like your favorite wallpaper, you admire
from afar.
She is a beautiful storm approaching. You can't
hear a thing but if you were to look inside her
riotous eyes, you would lose yourself inside
the winds of her soul, the whistling of
hurricanes blowing right through you. Her
love can rip you apart...then put you back
together again.
She is an ocean of depths, the weak at heart can
only wade through for fear of drowning inside
her. She is tragically soft and vulnerable
but she loves the hardest, the deepest.
It's the only way she knows how to be.
And waits only for someone to notice, and still,
she waits only for someone to see. -N.R.Hart

Our love didn't have to
make sense.
Our souls understood
one another
and that's all that mattered.

-N.R.Hart "soulmate poem" ©2018

She made me feel
like something special.
It was the way she looked
at me...
like I was the only thing
that mattered.
Like she couldn't take
her eyes off me.
Like I was something
worth seeing.
No one ever looked at me
the way she did.

-N.R.Hart   "The Way She Looked At Me"

This universe has its
own plan you see
and it seems to know
what you mean to me
every night when I
look up above
and write about
the stars and the moon
it's really about how
I can't forget you.
-N.R.Hart

A Spring Season

"Only the heart knows what
it did for love.
N.R.Hart

There was something
different about you
but I wasn't sure
what...
you were all these
feelings...
I never felt before.
-N.R. Hart

You made me love you

And, I thought to
blame you...
for this madness in my eyes
the hunger in my bones
the way my soul is in love
with your soul.
I am addicted to the way
you make me feel.
You are my best friend...
you became my everything.
And, I thought to blame
you...
you made me love you.

—N.R.Hart

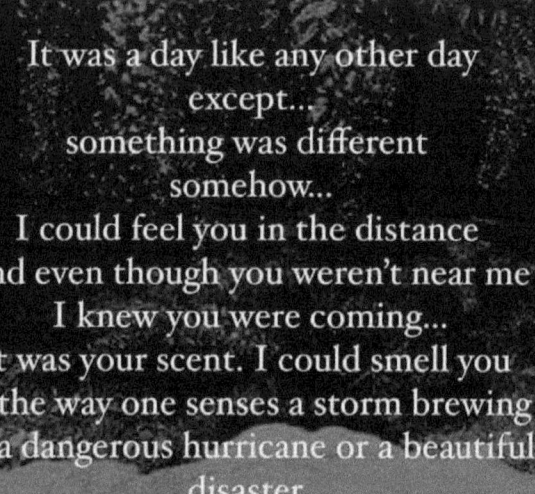

It was a day like any other day
except...
something was different
somehow...
I could feel you in the distance
and even though you weren't near me
I knew you were coming...
It was your scent. I could smell you
in the way one senses a storm brewing
or a dangerous hurricane or a beautiful
disaster.

N.R.HART "BEAUTIFUL DISASTER" ©

Truth is, he never knew how to handle her.
From the very beginning their chemistry together was explosive.
Something about her made him lose control and he didn't like losing control.
And this is what scared him the most.
-N.R.Hart

Her mind said
"seduce me"
her heart said
"make love to me"
and her soul said
"fuck me".

-N.R.Hart

"Conversations in the dark"

Elements of the Universe

I know this thing we have
is fragile and somewhat
complicated a
rare love forged
by longing fired by desire
an unexplained
force so when
you come for me just know
it is useless fighting the
elements of the universe.
—N. R. Hart

We had it all, didn't we...?
We were friends and lovers
we were soulmates and twin flames.
And, it has been impossible at times.
This being too much to each other.
This feeling too much...loving too much.
A love that was bigger than both of us.
A love that we didn't know what to do with.
A love that was everything...
Because the hardest loves are also the
greatest loves.
And, it was the friendship in us
this 'best friend' friendship that saved
us from each other every time...
Because the only thing scarier than
staying is leaving, so we stay.
And, we fight.
For the friendship, for the love, for us.
For everything...
Because it is hard, so very hard to imagine
a world...without 'us' in it.
-N.R.Hart "Everything"

He touched her
in places
where no one else
could reach...
the deepest
most familiar parts
of her naked soul.

-N.R.Hart

One look one word
one touch
and you happen
to me
all over again.

-N.R.Hart "All Over Again"

Heaven and Hell

She's the girl
you can't stop thinking
about
the girl you won't ever
forget.
She's under your skin
casting earthly spells.
She's inside your thoughts
you can no longer escape.
She's your clear blue
heaven
and your fiery red hell.
She's everywhere in you.

-N.R.Hart "heaven & hell"

I miss you

I miss saying hi to you.
I miss the way we used to talk.
I miss our long car rides
together.
I miss how I would jump
on your lap whenever I saw you.
I miss our laughter together.
I miss our texting sexting
all of it.
I miss your eyes
the way they looked at me.
I miss our hot wild sex.
I miss touching you,
 kissing you.
I miss how I loved you. I miss you.

—N.R.Hart ©2015

I want you next
to me
beside me inside me
your body close
all flesh and bone
feel your hands
on me
your heart beat.
I want you now.
I want you all the time.

—N.R.Hart

In His Kiss

He looked her in the eye
grabbing her by the hair
with his other hand on
her throat
pulling her towards him
so roughly so sweetly
so intently...
his mouth crushing down
hard on hers
she was overcome by his dominance
his lust
his desire.
Every inch every line every curve
he took...
It was all love and fire.
It was all in his eyes.
It was all in his kiss.
She was his.

—N.R.Hart "in his Kiss"

She just wants to forget
about life for awhile.
She chose you because
it's easy with you.
She feels safe enough
to show you her
vulnerability.
You can speak the language
of the stars with her.
Take her to places
she's never been
without ever leaving.

N.R. Hart

I believe in the laws
of attraction.
I only know when you are
attracted to someone
and they to you...
It is impossible to be
sitting next to them
and not be touching
them.
So if by chance you feel
the slightest whisper
of a touch from me...
you will know for certain
that I had no choice
other than to touch you.

-N.R. Hart "laws of attraction"©

You will have to peel
my body from yours
our souls
cannot be apart
you see, they have been
connected
from the very start
so when you go
just know
my soul goes with you.
-N.R.Hart

And, it's a mystery
just sitting next
to you...
I don't know how
not to keep
falling...
madly in love
with you.

-N.R.Hart "mystery"

It was your eyes
I could not look away from.
Your eyes that seemed
 so familiar.
Like mirrors to my soul...
The ones that see right
through me.
The ones that know the real me.
The ones that can always feel me.
I see my own reflection
staring back at me.
The side I don't show anyone
but you.
The side that knows you too...
Because, even if I tried
to explain us,
they would never understand.
And, sometimes even
we don't understand it.
We just know we need it.

-N.R.Hart "Need"

She wasn't asking for the world,
not really...
to feel the sunshine in her hair
good music, a strong cup
of coffee
poetry books and him.
She wanted him.
His undivided attention...
to be the object of his affections.
She wanted his stupid jokes.
His beautiful mind.
His lips on hers.
And, she wonders to herself...
is she the only one that feels
this way...every day?
Because, girls like her they know
of no other way to love.
It takes everything they have.

—N.R.Hart "object of his affections"

Sometimes...
our own love story
is right in front
of us
and we are too blind
to see it.
And, sometimes we find
our soulmate in a best
friend.
And, sometimes it has
been right there... all
along.

-N.R.Hart "Love Story"

You are the love
that came without warning
much like a violent wind
ripping through the ravines
of my soul
leaving me breathless
and shaken.
-N.R. Hart

I want to feel the heat of passion the madness of lust the pounding of my heart. I want only this and I want it with you.
N.R.Hart

She only knew she needed
his hands on her
touching her feeling her
destroying her in so many sweet ways.
She craved his rough possession
of her.
She wanted to be ruined.
She wanted to be his.

—N.R.Hart

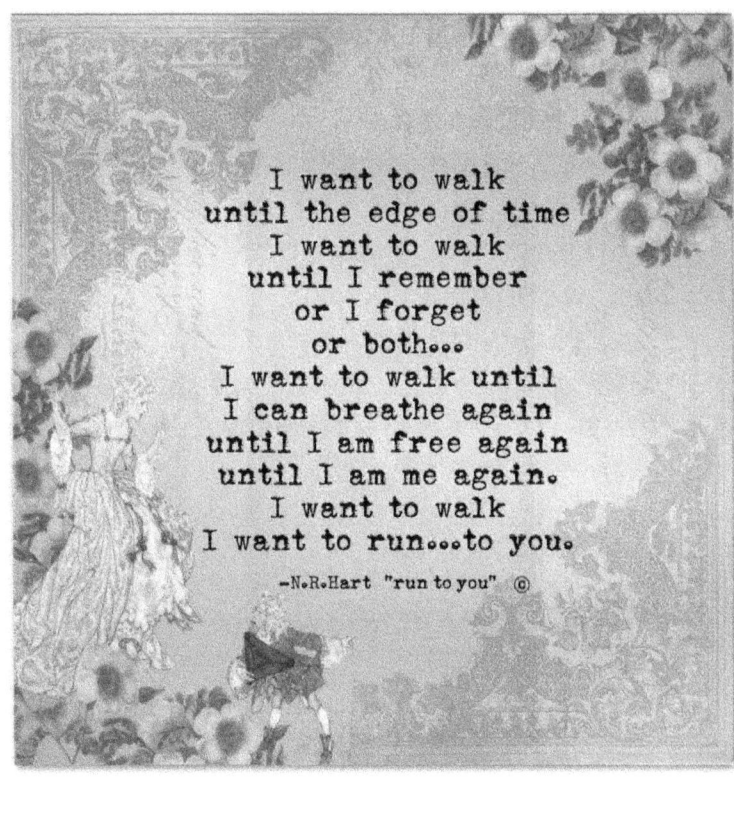

Hold my hand.
I felt safe with you
that day you held on tight
leading me through
the woods
pinning me up against trees
your lips planted on mine
when it was just you and me.
Can we go back?
Hold my hand again.
Take me there.

—N.R.Hart   "Take me there" © 2014

I just like being
with you
it doesn't matter what
we do.
Being close to you is all
I want.
Your nearness is all I need.
Have you ever just craved
being with someone?
That someone is you.
I miss you terribly
and I don't know what
to do.

-N.R.Hart "crave"

I can't tell you
the exact moment
I fell in love with you
but, maybe it was the way
your eyes looked different
that day
they seemed a little
deeper and your smile
a little sweeter
how your touch lingered
on me
a little longer
because, everything felt
different that day...
and I knew I would never
be the same again.

-N.R.Hart "the day I fell in love"

The one that makes you
the craziest
the saddest, the happiest
the maddest you have
ever been...
the one that makes it
hard for you to breathe
or even think clearly
the one that makes you
feel everything...
don't be too alarmed
my darling,
it only means they are
the One.

-N.R.Hart "the One"

You come to me like something
I never knew was missing
but so desperately needed.
You come to me like the pristine
heavens opened up and dropped
you into my arms.
Like two lovers fated by stars
and destiny colliding upon
impact.
You come to me as a universe
of love unveiled in your dark
mysteries.
You come to me as the very heart,
the very soul of me.

—N.R.Hart "Twin Flame, you come to me"

I don't know how else
to explain it other than
we work, we just work
the two of us....
and it's natural
and insanely hot
and completely mind-blowing
all at once.
The sweet bliss in the knowing
we just "get" one another
the utter comfort of being
in the presence of
a soulmate.
Because, it was just understood
between the two of us...
that I was your favorite person
and you were mine.

-N.R.Hart "understood"©

Your hands running
through my hair
your touch racing
through my bloodstream
lovesick
unrequited love...
empty echoes inside
the swollen chambers
of my heart.
This world is on fire
with you inside me
and no escape
out of my mind.

-N.R.Hart "unrequited love"

I just wanted
to be something
you needed
in the way that
I needed you.
Like something as
simple
as breathing...
and just as necessary.

-N.R.Hart "Breathing"

"Twin Flame"

You will know
the moment
you come upon your
Twin Flame.
They will start
a fire in you
that will not die.

-N.R.Hart ©2018

A Summer Season

"The beauty in her craves
the beast in him.

N.R.Hart

Beauty and her Beast

"She was a beauty who never wanted the prince she always wanted the beast."

-N.R.Hart

We went crazy
for each other
fell in way too deep
loved too hard and
got lost in the debris
but tell me...
weren't we the most
beautiful disaster
you ever did see?

—N.R.Hart

Beautiful disaster
©2016

"Bad Boys"

She likes the bad boys or the ones who pretend
to be bad. Because underneath that tough-guy
exterior that wolf-like glare is the most
vulnerable of souls.
Once uncovered by gentler hands their souls
are the deepest color of midnight.
The fullest moon. N.R.Hart ©
They are the ones who will love you so fiercely,
you will fall madly in love even before you knew
what hit you.
You can't help but feel possessed by them, every atom
of their love exploding inside you.
They don't scare easily. They won't run for cover.
Their hands strong enough to carry you.
Their arms big enough to shelter you.
They may look like a bad boy, they may act like
a bad boy, all hands and heart, all danger and charm
and yet, they possess the deepest kiss,
the hardest love.
They are unabashedly unafraid to love you...
And, you won't likely ever forget how you were
loved by them. Yes, she is just a good girl
who likes bad boys. -N.R.Hart

"

He set her on fire then watched as she went down in flames...Yet she couldn't help going back for more because some are just worth burning for.

N.R. HART "BURN" ©

Burning stars

She couldn't fully
explain
his effect on her...
she only knew that he
made her feel
like no one else could.
He made her see stars
and how she was
burning and dying
at the same time.
He made her feel alive
and she needed that feeling...
She needed him.

—N.R.Hart "burning stars" ©2016

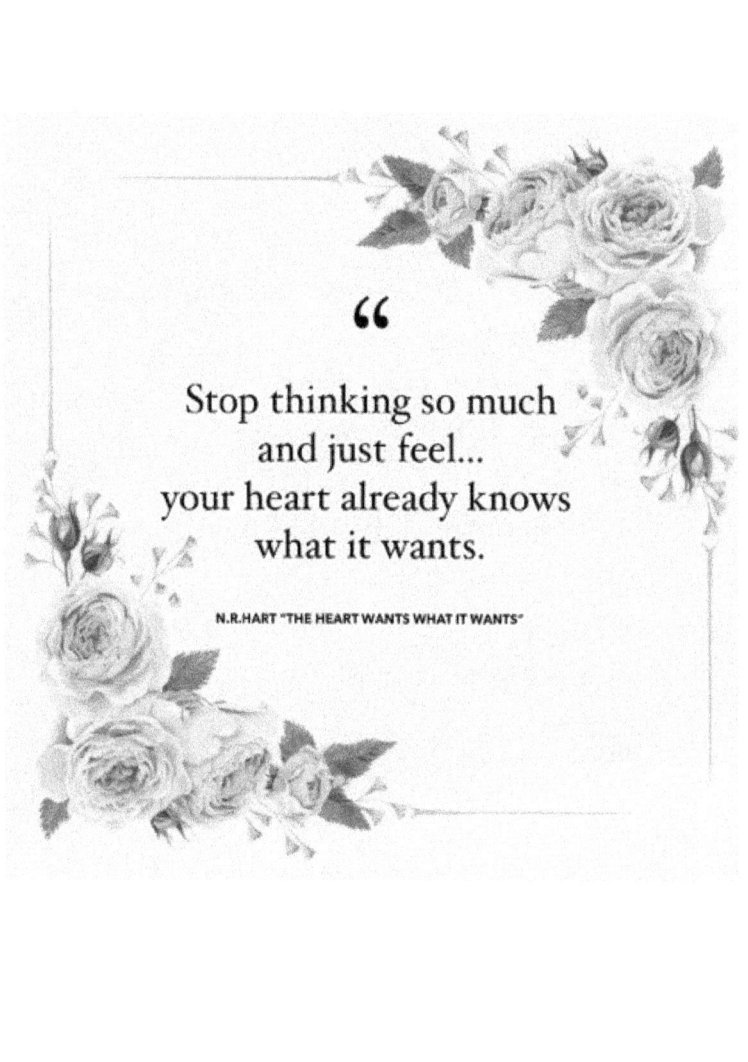

> Stop thinking so much and just feel... your heart already knows what it wants.

N.R. HART "THE HEART WANTS WHAT IT WANTS"

There was a certain
madness
in loving you
that made it quite
real;
it made it quite true
it was the most I had
felt;
loving you.

—N.R.Hart "madness"

It was the exchange of power
and how his strength made
her weak
she felt safe and somehow still
in danger
she felt free and yet, bound to him.
she was completely captivated
by the way he made her feel.
It was when he said "I can take what I
want when I want."
and she knew right then
she could never deny him.
How she craved his pure dominance over
her
surrendering fully to a man
who was both firm and gentle
with his love.
he thrilled her to the bone
bringing her to her knees
and, how it terrified her
all the ways she wanted...
she needed...to please him.

—N.R.Hart "dominance"

I loved you with my eyes
because they only saw
the good in you.
I loved you with my mind
because I never ran
out of words for you.
I loved you with my heart
because it still beats your
name.
But mostly, I loved you with
my soul.
Because my soul always
remembers.
Because my soul never forgets.

-N.R.Hart, I Loved You With My Soul

Forever People

Why is it so easy
for some to
walk away...
When I pick my people
to love they are
my forever people
here to stay.

N.R. Hart

There is a certain madness
in falling in love with
someone's mind
you know there will be
no one like them again
in the way they intrigue you
how they turn you on
as you lose yourself
inside their heads
being held captive by
their words
as if they own every bit
of you. -N.R.Hart

It was one of those
hot summer days
sitting so close
our skin sticking together
slipping into one another
your hands in my hair
my mouth stained with
your kiss
our bodies glistening
we were floating on air
as we caught our breath
and it was all such
a beautiful mess.

-N.R.Hart "beautiful mess"

Knight on a horse

You came out of nowhere
sweeping me off my feet
hearts on fire
flames everywhere
Lost lovers reunited!
Afterwards, I heard you say
"And, that's how it's done".
Like a knight storming in
on your horse getting the girl
saving the day.

-N.R.Hart "Knight on a horse, Lost Lovers" ©

"

She needs his hands on her
owning her
protecting her
loving her...
A sharp sting to her flesh
leaving his mark
reminding her she is his.

N.R.HART

Oh, how he wanted her
she had somehow gotten
underneath his skin
the taste of her
still in his mouth
breathing her in and out
she lives inside him
a savage love;
pure raw addictive
he craved her badly
but even more than that
he loved her. Madly.
-N.R.Hart

You were made up
of all my favorite
feelings...
a familiar soul
eyes to get lost in
and hands that felt
like home.
You were the safest
place
I have ever known.

-N.R.Hart "safe place"

Ride like the wind

There are some days I am busy
convincing myself
I am not still waiting
for you...
but when night falls
and the stars are out
they shine brighter
when I think of you.
I would drop everything
back then, as I would now...
just to have one of those moments
again with you.
No questions asked
I would hop into that car
of yours
kiss you hard....
And, ride like the wind.

-N.R.Hart "ride like the wind"

© 2013

I walk these shores
where we walked last...
and I recall the way
your eyes looked that day
how they carried the entire
ocean
and how I was drowning
inside them...
salted waves of longing
crashing down hard upon me.
How deeply I crave you
and I wonder...
Was there life before you?
Was I barely breathing at all?
Because all I remember is you
and how you felt...
and the persistent taste
of your kiss.
How this love haunts me.
How this love runs through me hard
like the wind, the rain and the sea.

-N.R.Hart "sea of love" ©

He came to her just like
she knew he would.
He always comes to her when
she calls out to him.
A siren's call.
A lover who can read her thoughts.
A lover who can feel her soul.
She became vulnerable with
each touch of his hand
he was claiming every inch of her.
He was claiming all of her.
She let him love her
so fiercely...so tenderly...
so completely.
For souls know when they are home.
For souls have a secret language
all their own.
Because, she belonged to him
and he belonged to her
and it was there...
they made their world.

-N.R.Hart "sirens call" ©

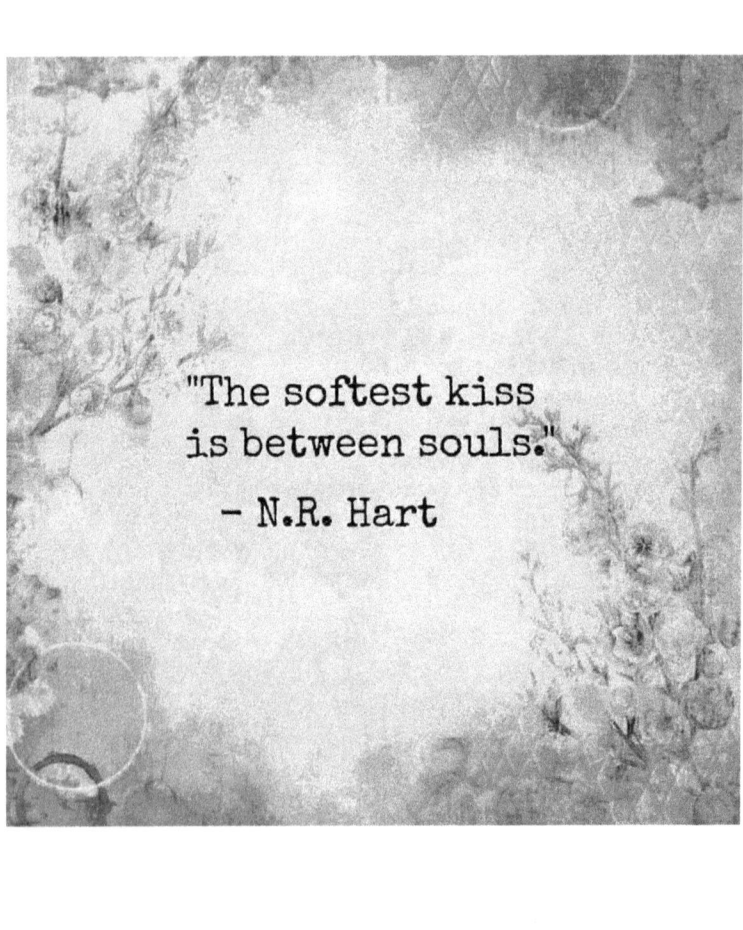

Spellbound

We have our own little world
you and I...
and how everything stops
including time.
I feel your words touching me
whispering things
demanding things
your sweet deadly words.
I fall apart. I fall for you.
And, I am under your spell
again.
My only desire is for you
to possess me
to dominate me. Make me yours.
Feel me come undone
in your hands...
how I surrender to you.
My mind my body my soul.
Love me. Take me. All of me.

-N.R.Hart   "Spellbound" ©

She is worth the risk
you love her chaos
how hard she loves you.
She never could deny
her love for you...
then why are you
not as brave as she?
and still she is your weakness
how alive she makes you feel
your own personal kryptonite
it's why you can't let go
with your heart of armor
and your hands of steel.
-N.R.Hart "Superman"

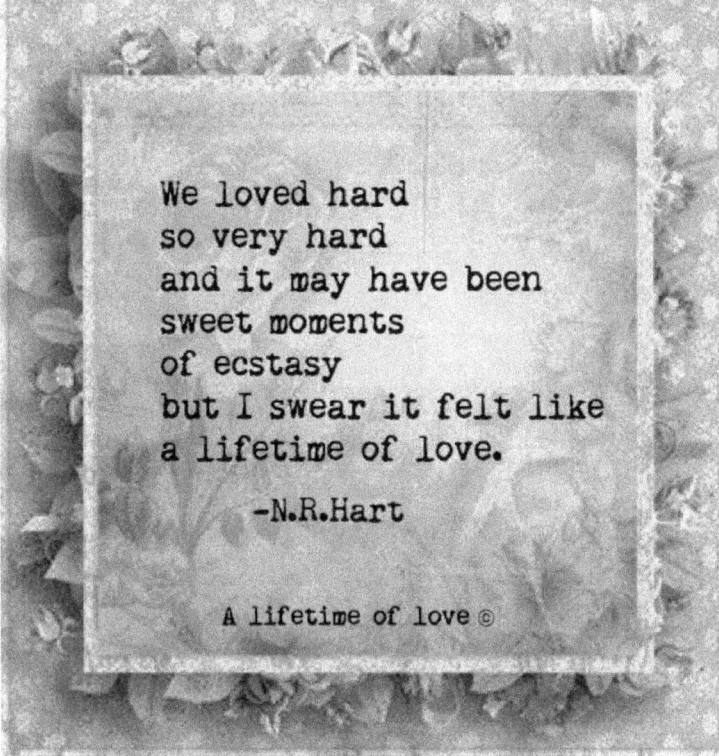

We loved hard
so very hard
and it may have been
sweet moments
of ecstasy
but I swear it felt like
a lifetime of love.

-N.R.Hart

A lifetime of love ©

"Temptation"

He was like the devil
himself
tempting her in all ways
of heavenly sin.
The hell with everything
else...
they both knew they couldn't
resist each other.
She would rather have
the 'oh well' than the
'what if' with him...
Everything else be damned.

    -N.R.Hart ©

> If it is between
> the sheep and the wolf;
> go with the wolf.
> He will love you
> in the tenderest
> but fiercest of ways.
>
> —N.R.Hart

I thought it was beautiful
the way we fell
for each other quietly
like a soft rain
And in the next moment
we were trembling
like thunder.
-N.R.Hart "Poetry and Pearls"

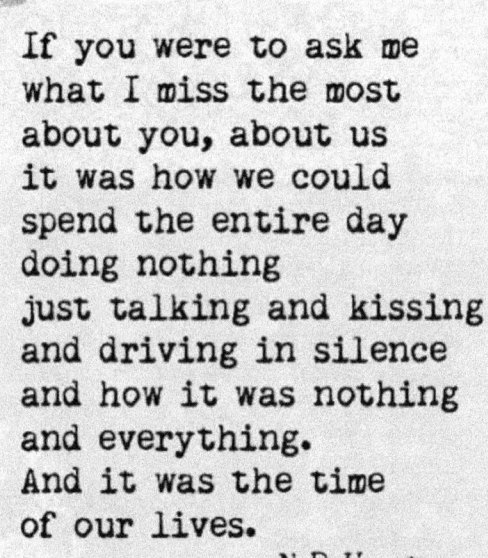

If you were to ask me
what I miss the most
about you, about us
it was how we could
spend the entire day
doing nothing
just talking and kissing
and driving in silence
and how it was nothing
and everything.
And it was the time
of our lives.
　　　　　　-N.R.Hart

"Time of our lives"

"Twin Flames" (a paradox)

Meeting your twin flame will be one of the strongest, most powerful connections in your life. And, it may also be the most confusing and difficult ones too. There is only one twin flame and not everyone has met theirs in their lifetime.

But, you will know immediately once you come across them, the connection is so pure and fiery, they will feel strangely familiar to you. It will almost be an out-of-control feeling. One that scares you and excites you at the same time.

You are left breathless...and yet, there is a stillness inside of you. There will be complete chaos...and yet, you will feel at peace.

Almost as if you cannot be apart, but you cannot be together, either.

You cannot live with them but you cannot live without them.

You feel as though nothing can replace the emptiness they leave behind and they sense this same emptiness...and they are on their way back to you...every time.

Even though the world keeps trying to pull apart what the universe knows should be together.

They can reunite many times in a lifetime.

Twin Flames can be the biggest paradox because they are literally the other half of your soul in another person...fighting to exist apart....And, simply cannot. -N.R.Hart

Wolf matters

To her, he seemed
experienced
in mind matters
in love matters
in wolf matters...
he made her soul
dance.
Her breathless heart
never stood a chance.

—N.R.Hart ©

You were always the moon

I always thought you were
the rain
all heartache and hurricanes
until I noticed you were
actually the sun
so beautiful and blazing
only to realize you were
the moon all along...
sweet dreams and love
cradling my delicate storms
in your strong hands
because you were big like
the sky
and yes, you were always
the moon.

-N.R.Hart "you were always the moon"

She wants a strong hand
and a tender touch
one who can protect her
like a beauty and love her
like a beast.

-N.R.Hart "Beauty and her Beast" ©

Her eyes searched
his...soulfully
she never needed
answers to love
only to look into
his eyes...
and know that he was
feeling it too.

-N.R.Hart

An Autumn Season

"You and I, our souls forever tangled
like the wolf is to the moon…"
N.R.Hart

Seasons of the Heart

I wanted to kiss you a little deeper,
long before the autumn leaves turned crisp
and
the winter's chill settled
into my bones.
I wanted to hold you a little tighter,
long before the spring flowers bloomed
tasting of your sweet kiss
and everything I can no longer feel.
I wanted to look into your eyes a little
longer,
long before the summer stars
in your gaze went out
one by one,
leaving me in the dark.
I wanted all these things, long before you
became a memory
one I take out...to remember, to hold, to live
inside again.

-N.R.Hart "Seasons of the Heart"

You don't know this but
I secretly live and breathe
for the texts from you...
they make my day
my heart starts pounding
when I see your name appear
and suddenly I am flushed
over these words
from you...
'where are you right now?'
because this question
holds infinite possibilities
because this question
excites me to no end.
And, my answer is always
the same.
I would be anywhere
with you.
And, anywhere is everywhere
when I'm with you.

-N.R.Hart "Everywhere...With You"

She was in danger of loving
him too much,
she was helpless
the way he could pin her down
using only his eyes
how her breathing changes
anticipating his touch
and the way his hands could
break her into soft wild
pieces
each screaming his name
oh, how she falls every time
over these quiet treacherous
things and how she keeps falling
again and again. -N.R. Hart

There are some hands
that feel so familiar
so strong and safe
as they lay inside
yours...
and these are the hands
you never let go of.

-N.R.Hart ©

How do you keep two souls apart when they felt so familiar from the very start.
   -N.R. Hart ©

She wanted to show him
that he had always
been worthy of love...
for within every beast
is just a man who desires
to love and be loved...
by his true beauty.

-N.R.Hart "Beauty and her Beast"

There is this thing that happens
when you meet the one that
changes your breathing
and nothing ever feels the same again
you breathe differently
think differently
act differently
you are consumed by thoughts
of them
you look for them
in the eyes of strangers
a glimpse of that familiarity
the one that makes you feel
like everything now makes sense
because before them...
nothing made sense
and now everything feels familiar
with them
like they built a home in you
A home that you carry around with you.

    -N.R.Hart "home"

She has this way of
knowing your
feelings
even before they've
had a chance
to surface ... It was
as if she could
feel your soul
long before you do.
-N.R.Hart

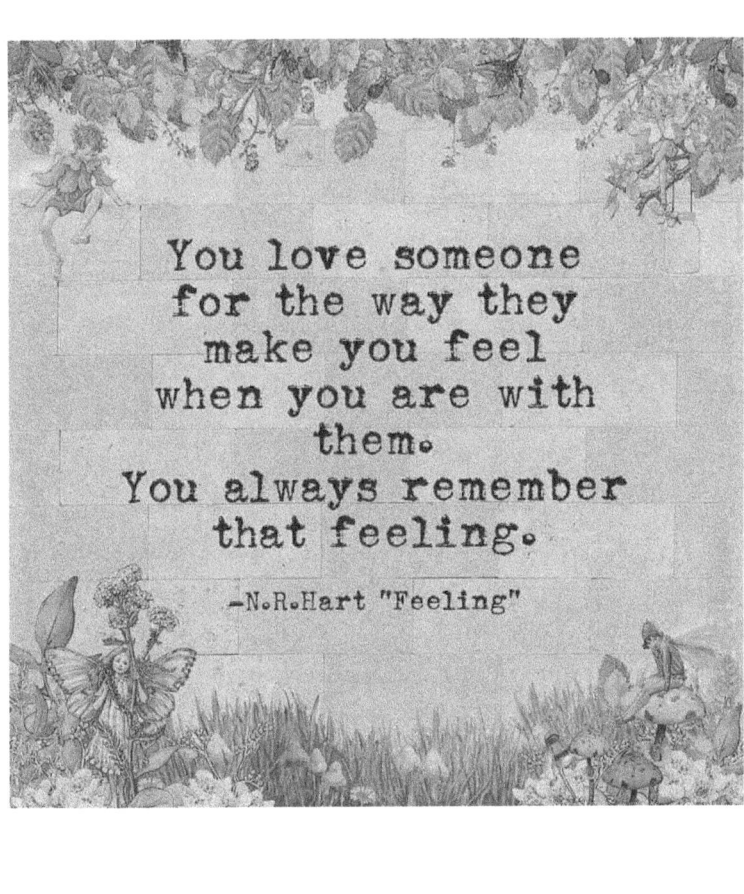

She will be the girl
who loves you like no
other.
The girl whose kiss still
lingers
on your lips.
The girl whose memory
refuses to fade away.
She will be the girl
you won't ever
forget.
The one who got away.
She will be forever...
that girl.

—N.R.Hart "forever that girl"

oh my darlings,
beautiful things are
never perfect
same for you and me.

-N.R.Hart

She felt his eyes
on her
always watching
over her
and then she knew
being haunted was
for the living too.

-N.R.Hart "Haunted"

Heartbreaker

She is the type of girl that makes you uncomfortable, isn't she?
One of the rare ones that has this otherness to her...
as if entire worlds are happening inside her you know nothing of.
She makes you nervous because she makes you feel and that scares you.
She is different from the others and you don't know quite how to handle her.
Never underestimate her she will outsmart you at every turn.
She wants the one who can challenge her keep up with her passion and intelligence.
She craves deep intimacy and connection.
She craves to be alive.
And, this scares the hell out of you because she demands more of you.
She demands all of you.
Some are intimidated by her and yet she is perfectly fine being by herself.
Her aloneness is her strength not her weakness.
She doesn't need you....only if she wants you.
She has been described as a heartbreaker and yet, she will break her own heart loving you.
Only play with fire if you do not fear the flame.
She is not afraid to burn for what she loves. —N.R.Hart

It's been so long
so very long
since I have been with
you...
held you and kissed you.
I don't know how it is...
you seem like a stranger
now that still feels like
home. And, I miss you so.

-N.R.Hart "home"©

I will come for
you... even
if we are
worlds apart
I will always
love you...and
I will come for you.
　　-N.R.Hart

I want you. I want us.
I love you. I love us.
It's true...I can go on
living without you.
I just don't want to.

"Romeo" letters to Juliet

-N.R.Hart (romeo & juliet) ©

I go back
to the places
we used to go
just to lose myself
there again ...
and find you.

— N.R. Hart ©

We are so close
so very close
I feel you here.
But, why are you
near
and still so far
away?

-N.R.Hart "near & far"

You and I will
always be unfinished
business...
like putting a bookmark
in our favourite story
highlighting the most
'unforgettable' parts
and picking up
where we left off
with neither of us
wanting to turn
the page...

N.R. Hart || bookmark

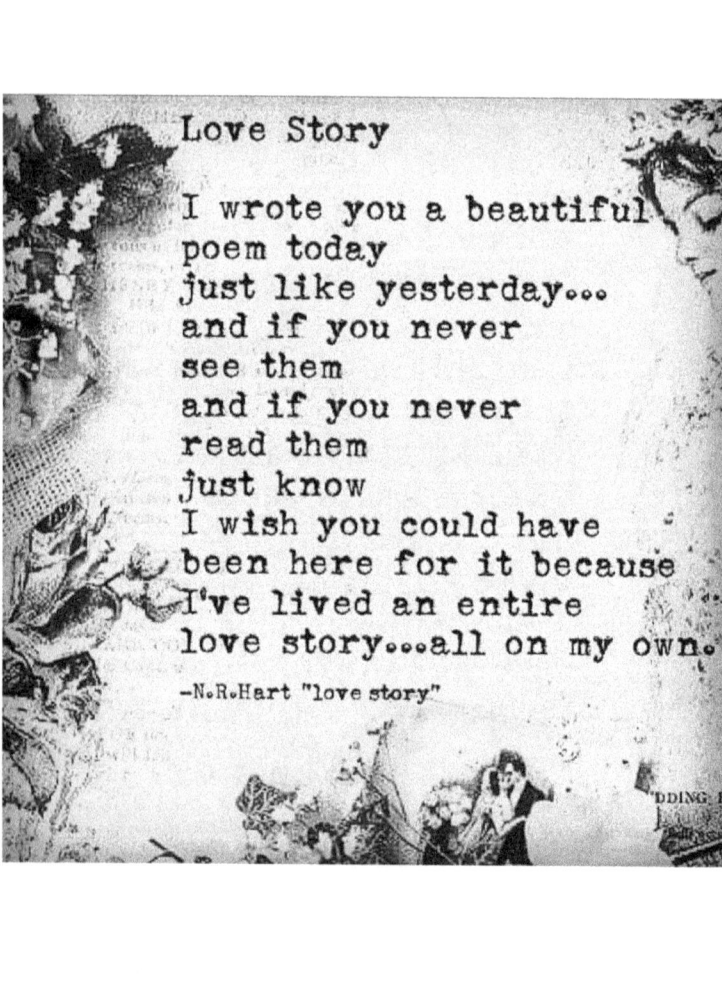

Love Story

I wrote you a beautiful
poem today
just like yesterday...
and if you never
see them
and if you never
read them
just know
I wish you could have
been here for it because
I've lived an entire
love story...all on my own.

—N.R.Hart "love story"

He wasn't prepared
for her love
maybe he was scared
no one had ever
loved him so
intensely before
he didn't know
whether to run
or stay for more...
N.R. Hart

Scent

I'm still wearing
your scent...
a fresh kiss
placed upon my lips
from the start
this fire
between us
never dies...
even when we are apart.

-N.R.Hart ©

You never know
how much you miss
someone
sometimes, it's just
a feeling inside you
that never goes away
like how you can't
breathe without them.
And, that's how you
know.
    -N.R.Hart

It was your scent
I couldn't quite forget
so utterly intoxicating...
And, how you have become
the biggest part of me
you are inside my bones
inside my veins...
I can't seem to make a move
without wanting every part
of you.
How I need my hands
on anything of yours...
just to wrap myself
in your warmth again
just to have you near me
again
just to remember again
just to breathe in your
sweet memory...again.

   -N.R.Hart (sweet memory)

You could see the way
they looked at each other
like nothing else existed
in the entire world
except the two of them.
They were all of it.
Best friends, lovers, soul mates.
They were something special.
But connections like that
are rare. And the love
between them so pure...
"It is very sad now...what
happened, they rarely speak."
Life. Life is what happened
and life can be
the saddest thing. -N.R. Hart

There are some moments
so special so everlasting
that words aren't even
necessary
like when I saw you again
after a long time
of missing you...
This was one of those times.

-N.R.Hart

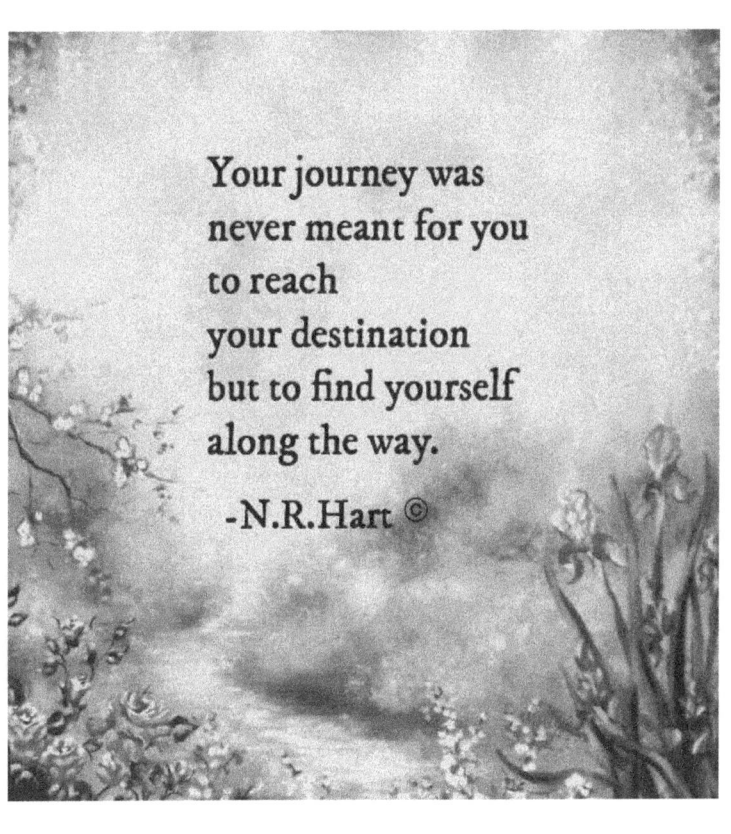

"Just come for me
and put an end to this misery."

– N. R. Hart, "come for me"

"You won't always recognize
the heroes of your story
while you are living it.
But you will understand
much later how you were
saved by them."

N.R. HART

Beauty and her Beast "Heroes" 2019

ABOUT THE AUTHOR

N.R.Hart started writing poetry at a young age and used her poetry as a way to express her innermost thoughts and emotions. A true romantic at heart, she expresses feelings of love, hope, passion, despair, vulnerability and romance in her poetry. Trapping time forever and a keeper of memories is what she loves most about the enduring power of poetry. Her poetry has been so eloquently described as "words delicately placed inside a storm." Poetry is here to make us feel instead of think; as thinking is for the mind and poetry is for the heart and soul. N.R.Hart hopes to open up your heart and touch your soul with her poetry.

"Poetry is not dead, it is alive
in the minds of those
who feel...instead of think."

N.R.Hart

More romantic poetry by N.R.Hart

Poetry and Pearls Vol I
Poetry and Pearls Vol II
Love Poems to No One

Connect with N.R. Hart:
Facebook@N.R. Hart, Author
Facebook@PearlsSlippingOffAString
Instagram@nrhartpoetry
Tumblr@nrhartpoetry

Lightning Source UK Ltd.
Milton Keynes UK
UKHW012013280721
387943UK00001B/132